WHEN I GROW UP
I WANT TO BE _____
A-Z Of Careers for Kids
Children's Jobs & Careers Reference Books

BABY PROFESSOR
EDUCATION KIDS

Speedy Publishing LLC

40 E. Main St. #1156

Newark, DE 19711

www.speedypublishing.com

Copyright 2017

A key part of our lives, when we grow up, will be working. We'll work to create things, to serve people, and to make the money we need in order to live. It's never to early to find out what we might do in our working life!

A VINTAGE PHOTOGRAPHER

NEW JOBS COME AND OLD JOBS GO

As the world and its economy changes, the careers that people can hope for change, too. Not long ago, a lot of young boys hoped to drive trucks or even taxis for a living when they grew up. Now the era of the driverless car is not that far away. Only fifty years ago you could make a good living making film for cameras, but now that field has collapsed as people have moved to digital.

Here are some jobs that look like they will need more and more workers in the coming years. If one of them looks like a job you might like to do, it's not too early to start thinking about the skills and experience you will need to get to do the job well.

A FINANCIAL MARKET ANALYST

FINANCE JOBS

Money continues to be centrally important in all businesses. Where is it? How much do we have? Can we pay the bills we owe? Are we making a profit? Companies will always need smart, detail-oriented people who can answer these questions.

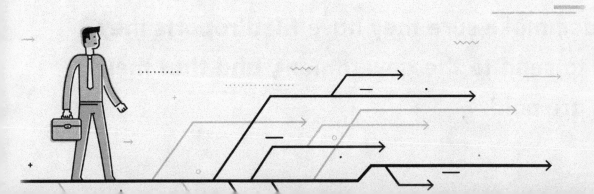

ACCOUNTANT

Businesses need an accountant to keep their books in order, make sure they have filed reports they need to send to the government, and that their taxes are paid.

Automated software can do some of those tasks, but not all. There is an ever-increasing number of businesses, and all of them need accounting services, annual audits, and financial planning to have the best chance of success.

FINANCIAL EXAMINER

Financial examiners work on the government side of finance. They keep an eye on banks, loan companies, and other bodies dealing with money to make sure they don't wander outside the law. Financial regulations keep evolving to make sure banks and similar bodies handle the money well and that the bad guys can't get at it.

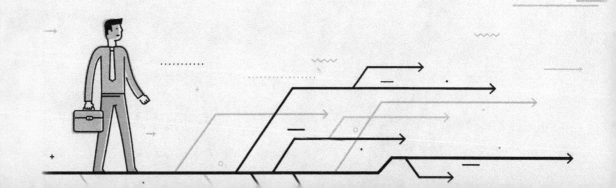

JOBS WITH PEOPLE

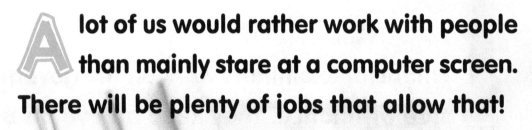

A lot of us would rather work with people than mainly stare at a computer screen. There will be plenty of jobs that allow that!

HUMAN RESOURCES SPECIALIST

HR people work for companies of all kinds. They recruit and interview possible staff and help fit the best work to the most suitable job. They help when problems arise in the workplace, design development plans so people can learn and grow at work, and make sure things like payroll and holiday schedules are handled well and accurately.

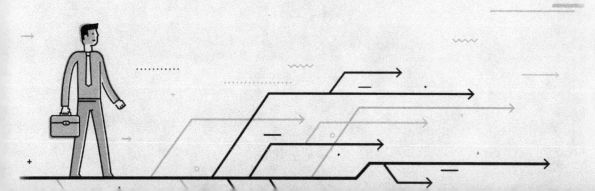

An HR person may travel to college campuses and job fairs to recruit new applicants, or even travel overseas for a big company that has branches in several countries.

INTERPRETER OR TRANSLATOR

If you have a gift for languages, or if you grew up speaking a second language at home as well as the majority language where you live, you have a skill-set that can help a lot of people

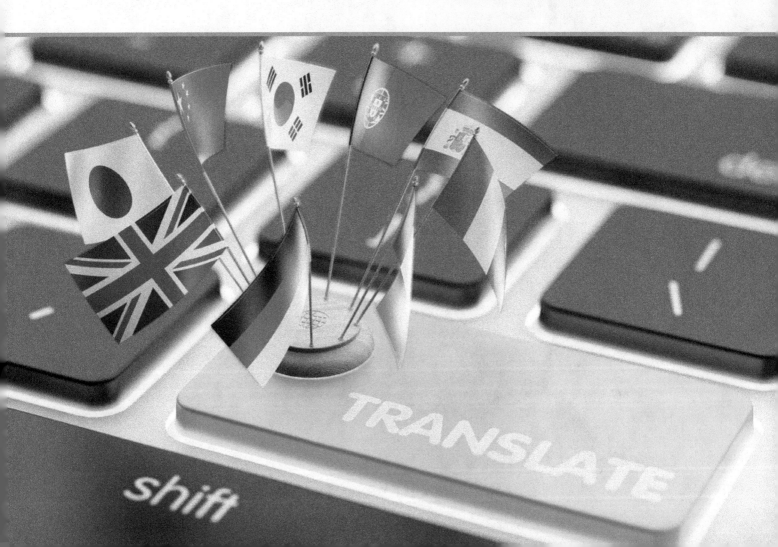

and lead to many jobs of different kinds. A lot of smart people have difficulty expressing themselves in spoken or written English, and rely on interpreters and translators to get what they want to say into a shape that their intended audience can understand.

A WOMAN INTERPRETING SPEECH OF PARTNER TO BUSINESSMAN AT INTERNATIONAL CONFERENCE

More and more commerce and political dealings require people skilled in more than one language to make sure that everybody comes away from a meeting, or signs a contract or an agreement, with the same understanding of what they are doing. There is a special need for sign-language speakers to help hearing-impaired people fully participate in their work and social lives.

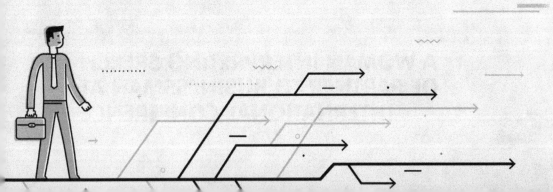

EVENT PLANNER

Companies hold events, schools and colleges hold events, groups hold reunions and memorial services, families have weddings and graduations to plan and enjoy. Event planners help people figure out all the things they need to get right so an event goes well and smoothly, and does not cost more than the people or the organization can afford.

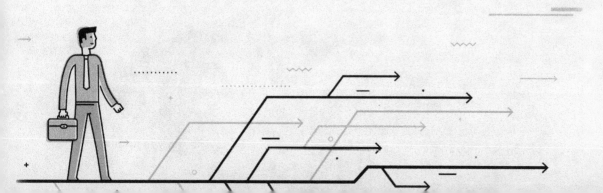

To do this job well you have to be able to keep many details in mind, understand how a complex project fits together, have a good sense of what is possible, enjoy dealing

with people even when they are tense and distracted, and be able to project a positive sense that everything is going to work out fine.

HEALTH-RELATED JOBS

The world's population is growing, and people are living longer. There is a growing need for healthcare workers, from support staff up to skilled surgeons. Where you fit in that world depends on your technical skills, how much you want to invest in studying and gaining expertise, and what sort of people you want to work with. Helping small infants and helping the elderly are not at all the same type of job!

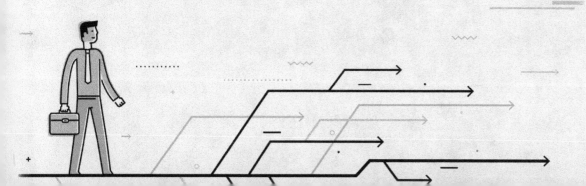

JOBS WITH LIVING THINGS

Some people want to work with living things, not with printouts or laboratory equipment. Fear not! There are developing jobs here, too.

URBAN AND SUSTAINABLE FARMERS

Most of our food is grown on big farms and brought to stores from long distances. But there is a growing need for urban farmers who can raise crops in the available spaces on rooftops or vacant lots, and deliver healthy foods a short distance to the people who want to eat it. Locally-grown food is often tastier and healthier than food that has to be grown so it can stand to travel long distances and sit on shelves for a long time.

VETERINARIAN

People love their pets and rely on the local vet to keep them healthy. Farmers rely on veterinarians to help prevent the spread of diseases that can destroy herds of cattle or sheep and ruin the farmer's income.

Vets do not have to train as long as doctors for people do, but they have to learn how to treat a wide array of creatures, from cart horses to cats to turtles.

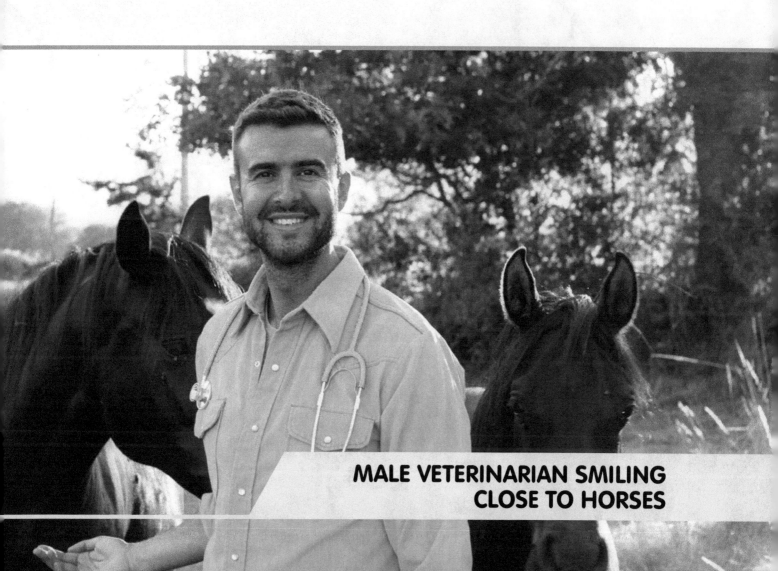

MALE VETERINARIAN SMILING
CLOSE TO HORSES

JOBS MAKING THINGS

• •

This is a physical world. People will go on needing real things to live inside, sit on, and drive in even as we are more and more in the computer age. What could you offer?

MASON

Masons build things out of brick, stone, and blocks of material. A lot of people who got into this line of work in the years after World War II are now retired or retiring, but the need for builders continues.

A MASON FINISHING A WALL

A mason has to be in good health, be good with tools, and have a good sense of design and spatial relationships.

The job does not require a lot of formal degrees, though, so it is an easier field to get into than many.

MASON LEVELING AND SCRAPING CONCRETE FOUNDATION WITH SQUARE TROWEL

CIVIL ENGINEER

Civil engineers design and manage the construction of major projects, like highways, bridges, dams, tunnels, airports and similar structures. The are called on to figure out how to rebuild or redesign aging systems that are wearing out, and to ensure that essentials like electric power and water are available to every person who needs them.

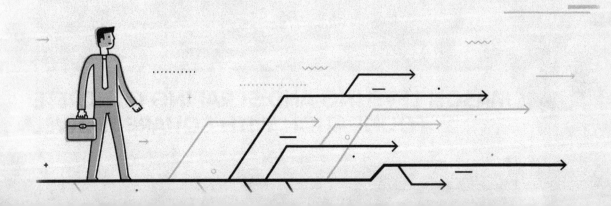

Civil engineers need good design sense, great ability with numbers, and also the skills to motivate and coordinate a large team of workers and specialists.

TECHIE JOBS

As technology gets more complex and covers more of our lives, it requires more and more people who know how to create and work with new things and maintain the stuff we already have.

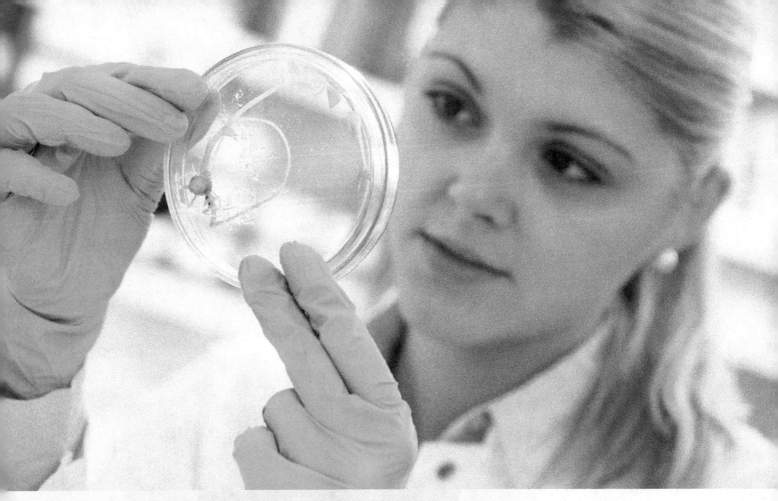

Here are some rising jobs:

BIOMEDICAL ENGINEER

This job takes a lot of training, and you would need to understand biology, human anatomy, computers, electronics, and lots more!

But you might be able to help research and design artificial organs, replacement limbs, and ways to provide hearing, sight, and speech to people who do not have those senses.

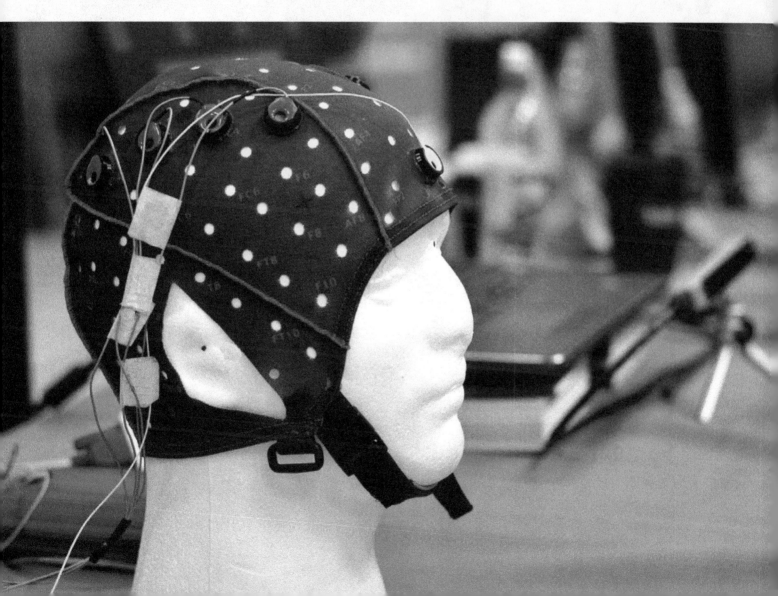

As people grow older, they need replacement hips and knees, cornea transplants for failing eyes, and pacemakers for stuttering hearts. Someone needs to design and create them!

SOFTWARE DEVELOPER

There is an unending demand for people who can build, extend, or maintain software applications for business, for entertainment, and even to manage the smart devices in your home.

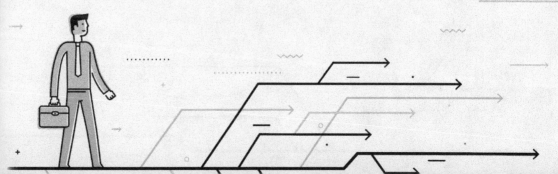

There is a confusing array of software languages you could choose from for the app you are to build, and lot of stuff that goes into even the simplest application. Fully-featured applications are usually the product of a whole team of developers and designers, not just one person.

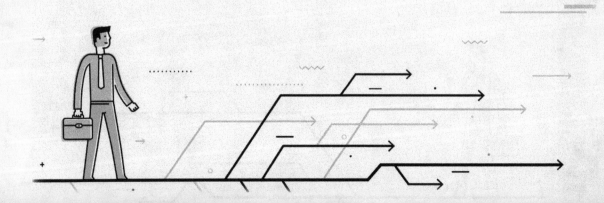

```javascript
        })
    }
    gridHeights()

    $(window).resize(function() {
        gridHeights()
    })

    $('.close-submenu').click(function() {
        $(this).closest(
        return false;
    })

    $('#contact-form').ajaxform({
        success: function(data,
            alert(data.message);
            console.log(form);
            if (data.status == 'success') {
                $(form).resetform();
            }
        }
    });

    $('.squares').isotope({
        // options
        itemSelector: 'li',
        layout: 'fitRows'
```

```javascript
    $('.squares').isotope('layout');
    $('.squares').isotope('layout');
```

However, there are lots of tools, even free ones, that make it pretty easy to design your first application right now. You can build a game or an app and run it on your own computer or smart phone, and

start learning the skills and work patterns that could make you a software development success.

THE JOB THAT FITS YOU

What do you want to work at after you are done with school? The answer to that question is different for every person. It depends in large part on what interests you.

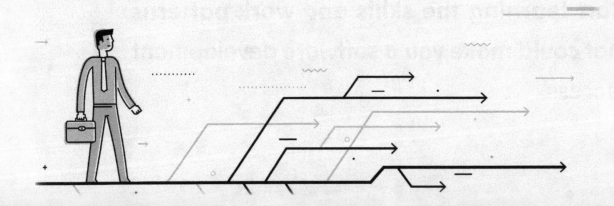

There's no point hoping to become an emergency-room nurse if you can't stand the sight of blood!

One way to start figuring out what sort of job you would like as a grownup is by trying out a kid-sized job now. The Baby Professor book Ka-Ching Ideas for Kids! has some good suggestions, and Can I Become a _____ Because I Like _____? can help you figure out what sorts of careers fit the kind of person you are.

Visit

BABY PROFESSOR
EDUCATION KIDS

www.BabyProfessorBooks.com

to download Free Baby Professor eBooks
and view our catalog of new and exciting
Children's Books

CPSIA information can be obtained
at www.ICGtesting.com
Printed in the USA
LVHW061532090920
665395LV00024B/2525